# The Sheppey Light Railway

## Peter A. Harding

R1 class 0-4-4T No. 1699 with articulated carriage set No. 513 and a parcel van in the Sheppey Light Railway bay at Queenborough Station. October 8th 1948.                    W. A. Camwell

Published by

*Peter A. Harding*

"Mossgiel", Bagshot Road, Knaphill,
Woking, Surrey GU21 2SG.
ISBN 0 9523458 7 0
First published 1984. Revised edition 2003.
© Peter A. Harding 2003.
*Printed by Binfield Print & Design Ltd.,
Binfield Road, Byfleet Village, Surrey KT14 7PN.*

# Contents

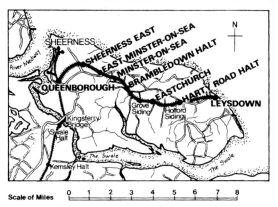

Scale of Miles

R1 class 0-4-4T No. 31696 leaving Sheerness East for Queenborough. November 14th 1950.　E. D. Bruton

Articulated carriage set No. 513 with a parcel van and R1 class 0-4-4T No. 31698 engine in the Sheppey Light Railway bay at Queenborough Station. March 4th 1950.　D. Trevor Rowe

2

# Introduction

The Sheppey Light Railway was one of the early railway lines to take advantage of the 1896 Light Railway Act and opened from Queenborough to Leysdown in 1901, traversing the sometimes lovely but often lonely Isle of Sheppey.

The line opened in 1901 with high hopes that it would bring prosperity to the island and transform Minster and Leysdown into popular seaside resorts. These hopes were never actually to materialise and the line became just a leisurely byway through pleasant countryside with numerous level crossings which were mainly operated by the train's guard. Things stayed that way until the line was closed completely in 1950.

Although it might not have brought prosperity to the island, it did serve local farmers and gave passengers a link to the main line at Queenborough. By retaining its light railway status throughout its lifetime, the Sheppey Light Railway held its slightly eccentric charm which, even today, well over fifty years after the last train left Leysdown, is still a fond memory to the older generation of islanders and railway enthusiasts alike.

I hope that this publication brings back one or two of those fond memories to the older generation and that the younger generation can capture some of that eccentric charm of a light railway from a bygone day.

R1 class 0-4-4T No. 1699 with articulated carriage set No. 513 and a parcel van at Leysdown Station. October 8th 1948.                                                                    W. A. Camwell

With the crossing gates closed against the road, the 10.55 a.m. for Leysdown waits at Brambledown Halt while the photographer captures the moment. December 2nd 1950. Dr. Edwin Course

3

# History of the Line

The Isle of Sheppey which lies to the south of the Thames estuary and is separated from the Kentish mainland by the firth of the Medway and the channel of the Swale, was first reached by railway on July 19th 1860 when the Sittingbourne & Sheerness Railway Company opened their single track line from Sittingbourne on the main London, Chatham & Dover Railway to Sheerness Dockyard in the Blue Town area of Sheerness via the Kingsferry Bridge and Queenborough.

The line was leased to the London, Chatham & Dover Railway who purchased it from the local Sittingbourne & Sheerness Company exactly five years later, on July 19th 1865.

In 1875 a short branch to Queenborough Pier was opened from Queenborough Station where at the time, with daily sailings to Flushing in Holland, it was hoped that Queenborough would develop into a major cross channel port.

A further short branch was added on July 1st 1883 when a line was opened from Sheerness Dockyard to the more residential area of Sheerness known as Mile Town. The station became known as Sheerness-on-Sea.

This railway development on the western side of the island still left the more remote villages and farms off the railway map and things were to stay like that until advantage was taken of the 1896 Light Railway Act to promote a line from Queenborough to Leysdown on the eastern side of the island.

The idea for this new line came not only from the influential Sheppey Board of Guardians who had taken a great interest in the Light Railway Act, but also from two wealthy landowners, Lord Harris of Belmont Park, Faversham who was also a well known Kent, Oxford University and England cricketer and Captain George Lindsey Holford who was the largest landowner on the island and the son of the millionaire Robert Holford.

The 1896 Light Railway Act was ideal for the type of line required to serve farming communities and less populated areas. It meant, in fact, a very basic railway with lighter permanent way, sharper curves, steeper gradients, speed restrictions, minimum signalling and station accommodation.

A body known as the Light Railway Syndicate who were incorporated in 1895 and were involved with the promotion of various other light railways were to organise and promote the new Sheppey Light Railway. Capital was set at £60,000 shares of one pound each and there were to be four directors, three from the Light Railway Syndicate and one other person to be nominated by them.

The engineer appointed to build the line was none other than the young and enterprising Holman Fred Stephens (later to become the celebrated Lt. Colonel Stephens) who was already making a name for himself in the world of light and minor railways. Stephens in fact managed several independent light railways from his office at Tonbridge in Kent, some of these lines being in other parts of the country. (For further information about Holman Fred Stephens see *The Col. Stephens Railways in Kent* by Peter A. Harding).

The Light Railway Syndicate was actually formed by Stephens and Edward I. W. Peterson who Stephens first became acquainted with while he was living in the Cranbrook area where he served as resident engineer to the Cranbrook & Paddock Wood Railway. Edward I. W. Peterson was a solicitor with a practice in Staplehurst and was the son of the Rector of Biddenden, the Rev. William Peterson.

Holman Fred Stephens

4

While Stephens was involved with the Cranbrook & Paddock Wood Railway he also came into contact with Lord Medway, one of that line's promoters, who later when hearing of Stephens' interest in the Sheppey project, gave him a letter of introduction to Lord Harris.

On receiving the letter, Stephens wrote the following letter to his father F. G. Stephens (who was a founder member of the pre-Raphaelite Brotherhood of artists and was later art critic to *The Athenaeum* magazine):

29th November 1896

My dear Dah,

I have a letter of introduction from Lord Medway to Lord Harris "re" a proposed line in Isle of Sheppey. You know so much better than I do how to manage these sort of things, how shall I address Lord Harris?

I write "My dear Lord Medway" because I know him, but I don't know Lord H. Shall I say "Sir" !! or "My Lord" ?

With best love to you both

Your affectionate son.

The original application put forward was for a standard gauge single line about 7³/₄ miles in length from the south side of Queenborough Station in an easterly direction through the southern marshes to a point on the east coast near Leysdown. No platforms needed to be provided at stopping places if, and so long as, all carriages in use were constructed so that the lowest step or footboard was not more than 16 inches above the ground. The maximum axle load was to be 15 tons, the speed limit to be 35 miles per hour and the rails were to be 60 lb. per yard.

Although the Sheppey Light Railway was never to form part of Holman F. Stephens independent group of light railways, while he was the lines engineer, he did in fact use headed note paper that was very much part of his Tonbridge set up.

---

# Sheppey Railway.

TELEPHONE: 223, TONBRIDGE.

TELEGRAMS:
STEPHENS, TONBRIDGE STATION.

ENGINEER'S OFFICE,

TONBRIDGE.

---

Before any enquiry was held it became quite clear that the route and the idea of no platforms did not meet with any great enthusiasm by local interested parties. In fact, Mr. John Copland, a Sheerness solicitor speaking on behalf of not only the Sheppey Board of Guardians but also the Sheerness Rural District Council and the Minster Parish Council voiced his opinion in no uncertain terms. A suggestion was then made that a route which included a station on the marshes adjoining the Halfway House Road (about a mile from the town of Sheerness) and another in Scocles Road, Minster would benefit the more fertile regions of the island. This suggestion plus various other wishes were taken into consideration by the promoters.

An inquiry was held before the Light Railway Commissioners, presided over by the Earl of Jersey at the town hall in Queenborough on Friday April 29th 1898 and was fully reported just over a week later in the May 7th 1898 issue of the *Sheerness Times & General Advertiser*. Part of the report mentioned the following:-

There was scarce a parish in the island which was not represented, despite the fact that the promoters of the proposed line had virtually disarmed opposition by the selection of the route which had been pressed upon them by Mr. John Copland and Mr. Charles Ingleton, as one calculated to secure greater benefits for the island, in preference to the route which the Engineer of the Light Railway Syndicate at first mapped out, which would have excluded Minster and Sheerness from all benefit from the opening up of the upper end of Sheppey to railway communication.

The inquiry was held by the Light Railway Commissioners, the Earl of Jersey, G.C.M.G. (who presided), Mr. G. A. R. FitzGerald, and Colonel Boughey, R.E., Mr. H. A. Stewart, Secretary to the Commissioners, being also present.

Mr. H. C. Gollan, barrister, & Mr. E. W. I. Peterson, solicitor, appeared for the promoters. The Mayor of Queenborough (Mr. J. E. Castle, J.P.) made excellent arrangements for the inquiry, and all who were present found comfortable seats. The Commissioners occupied the magisterial bench, and the council and officials of the Light Railway Syndicate sat at the table in front of the Commissioners. Public bodies of Sheppey were well represented. The Mayor (Mr. J. E. Castle, J.P.), the Deputy-Mayor (Mr. R. F. Halliwell), Alderman W. Pannell, and other members of the Queenborough Town Council were present, with Mr. W. J. Harris (Town Clerk); the Sheerness Urban District Council was represented by Mr. E. W. Brightman, J.P., C.C. (Chairman), Mr. J. T. French, and Mr. Vincent H. Stallon (Clerk); the Sheppey Board of Guardians by Mr. George Still (Chairman) and Mr. John Copland (Clerk); the Sheppey Rural District Council by Mr. Charles Ingleton (Vice-Chairman, who also represented the Minster Parish Council; the Eastchurch Parish Council by Mr. J. Bligh (Chairman); The Sheerness and Isle of Sheppey Chamber of Commerce by Messrs. Herbert Berry, W. J. Penney and A. A. Palmer. The Rev. R. H. Dickson, M.A., Mr. T. Horspool, and many other residents of the island were also present.

Mr. H. C. Gollan for the promoters stated that in response to certain requests they had decided to divert the line to the north so that it would leave Queenborough from the north side of the station and come within a mile of Sheerness at Halfway House Road and within half a mile of Minster at Scocles Road and rejoin the original alignment just south of Eastchurch, increasing the distance of the line by about a mile.

Mr. Holman F. Stephens, engineer to the promoters mentioned that after the advantages had been explained, he had no objections to the diversion and gave a full description of the revised route.

This scheme prompted an objection from Mr. W. J. Penney of the Sheerness Chamber of Commerce who felt that the diversion did not go far enough and suggested that the junction should not be at Queenborough but at a point near the Sheerness Dockyard and that the line should run through the Sheerness High Street to Halfway House Road.

The objection was over-ruled by the Commissioners who felt that it was not in the interest of making Leysdown more easily accessible from London. (It is interesting to note that this suggestion was later taken up in 1903 by the Sheerness & District Electrical Power & Traction Co. Ltd., who opened an electric tramway of 3ft 6in gauge from Sheerness Dockyard to Halfway House Road just north of what had by then become Sheerness East Station on the Sheppey Light Railway. Ironically, this electrical tramway was short-lived and only lasted until 1917.)

Mr. John Copland mentioned that he had approached the land owners on the diverted route, all of whom had given their consent to the line passing through their land. At this point, the Chairman thought this would be a fitting stage to read a letter he had received from Lord Harris.

6, Oxford Square, London, W.
April 26th, 1898

My Dear Jersey,
The promoters of the Sheppey Light Railway have asked me to be present at the inquiry at Queenborough on Friday, and if I thought that my evidence would in any way assist the Commission, I should of course go, but I feel that I should be unnecessarily taking up your time

if I was put into the box, for I could not speak from actual experience of the cost and inconvenience of the present long lead by cart from the other end of the island to the Chatham Railway. Any farmer at that end of the island could speak definitely upon these points; and, of course, it goes without saying that the railway would be of very great convenience to us. I should hardly imagine there are two opinions upon that point. There are, I believe, two opinions as to the alignment, and having considered both, I am in favour of that which goes more inland instead of along the line of the marshes, and which would, I should hope, be of convenience to the more populated parts of the island. If you think fit, I hope you will lay my letter before the Commission, and perhaps you will kindly explain to them that it is certainly from no want of respect to them that I have not gone down personally. I have instructed my Agent to support the proposal.

Your sincerely
HARRIS

Mr. Copland added that he too had received a letter from Lord Harris stating that he has instructed his agent Mr. George Webb to support him in the alignment, and like the other land owners, to raise no objection to the line going through his land.

Another important person who was also absent was Captain George Lindsey Holford, the island's largest land owner. Mr. Copland read a letter that he had received from Captain Holford, saying that he had also given his approval and had sent Mr. T. Horspool to represent him. Mr. Copland mentioned that he had also seen all the tenants and they had also given their consent. At this point it seemed that one of the tenants, a Mr. Goodwin of Harp's Farm raised an objection saying that the line would bisect his land. Mr. Copland said "You said you were agreeable providing you obtained sufficient compensation" to which Mr. Goodwin was understood to question this, but Mr. H. F. Stephens confirmed Mr. Copland's statement as to what took place.

At this stage, the Commissioners then heard from Mr. George Copus, manager of the Colne Valley & Halstead Railway in Essex who gave an account of the type of traffic the new line could expect.

The Commissioners seemed impressed with the new proposals and Lord Jersey stated that even though the new route was made so late, they would stretch a point on this occasion as there was no great objections, except in the case of Mr. Goodwin, which the promoters could no doubt meet, and added that the Commissioners had decided that they would recommend to the President of the Board of Trade to make an appropriate Light Railway Order. They felt that the maximum speed should be 25 miles per hour and not 35 as recommended by Mr. H. F. Stephens.

It was pointed out to the Commissioners that the Lambourne Valley Railway in Berkshire had been sanctioned at a speed of 25 miles per hour on 50 lb rails, so that it would be considered a reasonable request to permit a speed of 35 miles per hour on 60 lb rails.

Surprisingly, it took a year before the order was actually confirmed on May 3rd 1899 but the speed limit was to stay at 25 miles per hour and 10 miles per hour on approaching ungated crossings and sharp curves. The weight limit was to be 14 tons per axle and it was decided that the line should be fenced.

There had been a request at the time from the promoters for a possible railway hotel to be built at Leysdown, but no further action was taken on this proposal after Lord Jersey mentioned that building a hotel did not come under the Light Railway Act and the promoters would need to find an alternative way of obtaining permission.

The contractor appointed to build the line was William Rigby & Co., who had been regularly employed by the South Eastern Railway and had continued after the South Eastern Railway and the London, Chatham & Dover Railway had agreed in 1898 to work together under a management committee, known as the South Eastern & Chatham Railway (SE&CR) although both companies remained separate.

William Rigby made a start on the construction of the line a few days before Christmas 1899 when 40 men were employed under the personal supervision of Mr. T. Burt-Mason and the foremanship of Mr. Brotherton with a promise that the 40 men would soon be increased to anywhere from 150 to 200.

To mark the commencement of the construction work, an 'inaugural supper' was held on Wednesday January 10th 1900 by Mr. Marsh Pierson, a local farmer, and his brother Mr. W. Pierson of Faversham, at the Halfway House Inn where thirty guests sat down to a 'good spread', which was followed by the loyal toast and singing the National Anthem.

To help with the construction, William Rigby hired a locomotive from the London, Brighton & South Coast Railway at £2 per day. The locomotive was a 'Terrier' 0-6-0T No. 671 formerly called "Wapping" and designed by William Stroudley.

As the work progressed, stations were built at Sheerness East, East Minster-on-Sea, Minster-on-Sea, Eastchurch and Leysdown. With the exception of East Minster-on-Sea (which at first was only used on special occasions), all the stations had sidings while farm sidings were also provided at Brambledown (about ³/₄ mile on the Eastchurch side of Minster-on-Sea), Grove (1 mile beyond Brambledown), Holford (1 mile beyond Eastchurch), and Harty Road (about ¹/₂ mile from Holford).

The line received the official inspected by Major J. W. Pringle for the Board of Trade on Friday 21st of May 1901. Major Pringle reported that subject to the fulfilment of 7 requirements, plus the fact that should Eastchurch ever be used in the future as a passing station, it required a second platform, he recommended that the Board of Trade grant a certificate for the use of the light railway for passenger traffic under the train staff & ticket system.

After these requirements had been carried out, the Sheppey Light Railway was officially opened on August 1st 1901 and was worked from the outset on the company's behalf by the SE&CR.

The *Sheerness Times & General Advertiser* reported the event in their Saturday August 3rd 1901 edition as follows:-

### OPENING OF THE SHEPPEY LIGHT RAILWAY
**The First Train starts amid Cheering and a Salute of Fog Signals**

The Sheppey Light Railway is now an accomplished fact. Whether it will bring about all the prosperity to rural Sheppey that has been predicted remains to be seen, but there can be no doubt that it will be a great convenience to the residents, who are now brought into communication with the railway system of the United Kingdom by means of the South Eastern and Chatham Company's line.

The first train started from Queenborough at 9.5 on Thursday morning, and a goodly gathering assembled on the bridge which crosses the railway to witness its departure, while not a few took their seats for the initial voyage. The train was made up of six coaches — first and third class, there being no second-class on the line — and a luggage van. It was drawn by one of the small locomotives, which has been allotted for regular duty on the line. Mr. Howland, Station-Master at Queenborough, had gaily decorated the station with flags in honour of the auspicious event. Two or three officials made the first journey — Mr. Smith, Assistant-Superintendent of the S.E. and C.R. Company, and Mr. Durrant, Superintendent for the Faversham District, accompanying whom was Alderman W. Pannell, of Queenborough, who retired from the Company's service a few years since. Several local agriculturalists made the first journey, including Mr. T. Clifford, of Neats Court, whilst the Union officials were represented by Mr. G. Bligh.

Precisely to time, the passengers having taken their seats, the train steamed out of the station, amid hearty cheers, the waving of handkerchiefs, and the firing of fog signals, which had been placed along the line.

All along the route bunting was liberally displayed on the farms and also at the stations at Sheerness East, Minster, Eastchurch and Leysdown. There were several passengers waiting at Sheerness East, and on arrival of the train at Minster Mr. Charles Ingleton, J.P., and a number

8

of residents were in waiting to welcome the first passenger train, and to proceed in it to the Terminus. Mr. Thomas Horspool, who had made quite a brave show with bunting, met the train at Eastchurch, and at Leysdown Mr. C. A. Till and other residents were present to greet the passengers by the pioneer train. Altogether it was a memorable day for Sheppey.

A number of passengers met at the "Rose and Crown," Leysdown, and toasted "success to the Sheppey Light Railway".

The second train conveyed to Leysdown a number of South-Eastern and Chatham Railway officials, including Mr. Thompson, Superintendent of the Line, Mr. Wallis, Goods Superintendent, and Mr. Barker, Locomotive Superintendent. The officials, together with several gentlemen who had been connected with the construction of the line, afterwards lunched at the Royal Hotel, Sheerness to celebrate the opening of the route.

Mr. S. Salomon, manager of Abbott and Co's Boot Store, 37, High Street, Mile Town, presented each passenger who travelled by the first train with a souvenir card with the times of the arrival and departure of the trains.

The route is through some of the best scenery in Sheppey.

The luncheon that Mr. Copland proposed giving on the opening day of the Light Railway was, at the request of the Directors of the S.E. and C. Railway, postponed till the 9th, as they were unable to attend on the 1st. A special train will leave Victoria at 10.55 and arrive at Queenborough at 12.8. It will leave there at 12.13 and Sheerness East shortly after for the guests, and then after going to Leysdown will return to Sheerness East. The luncheon will be at the Co-operative Hall, Sheerness at 2.15 p.m.

As mentioned in the report, it was the intention of Mr. John Copland to hold a grand luncheon at the Co-operative Hall, Sheerness to commemorate the opening of the line on the actual day, so that both events might be synchronised, but as some of the officials of the SE&CR were unfortunately unable to attend, it was therefore decided to hold the luncheon on August 9th.

A special train left Queenborough at noon and Sheerness East a little later and then went on to Leysdown for a short stay where Mr. Robert Hilder of Sheerness took a photograph of the group on the platform. The weather was fine and the fertile countryside looked at its best. Later, the party of guests returned to Sheerness East Station where a number of traps were waiting to convey them to the Co-operative Hall

The party of guests who were photographed on the platform at Leysdown Station on August 9th 1901, having travelled by special train to commemorate the opening of the line. Author's Collection

9

This special occasion was fully covered in the Saturday August 10th 1901 issue of the *Sheerness Guardian* who listed the specially invited guests as follows:-

The representatives of the S.E.& C. Railway Company included Mr. Cosmo O. Bonsor, chairman of directors; Mr. Vincent H. Hill, general manager; Mr. Sheath, secretary; Capt. Tempest, Capt. Dickson, Mr. G. Wallis and Mr. Thompson, directors; Col. Boughley and Mr. A. D. Erskine, Light Railway Commissioners; Mr. E. J. Athawes, Stipendiary Magistrate, and Mr. J. L. Allen, his clerk; Mr. H. F. Stephens, Engineer of the Light Railway; Mr. Rigby, contractor; Mr. E. W. I. Peterson, solicitor to the Light Railway; Mr. Pressland, Engineer; Mr. A. W. Howe, J.P., C.C.; Mr. E. W. Brightman, J.P., C.C.; Mr. J. R. Brett; Revs. J. M. Tamplin, R. H. Dickson, E. W. Bartlett, W. Noblet, J. Castle, and R. B. Barber; Drs. Arrol and Caesar; Mr. Flood-Page (Queenborough); Mr. W. J. Harris (Sittingbourne); Members of the Board of Guardians; Sheerness Urban District Council and School Board; Queenborough Town Council and School Board; Mr. W. J. Penney (chairman) and directors of the Sheerness Economical Society; Mr. W. G. Tutt (chairman) and directors of the Sheerness Co-operative Society; and a large number of tradesmen of the town, making a total of about 160 persons.

After the Rev. J. M. Tamplin had given grace, Mr. Copland rose to speak amidst much cheering. He went on to say:-

That trains and time — not even on the Light Railway — waited for no one and he would therefore proceed at once to give the toast of "The King, Queen, and the rest of the Royal Family".

The toast having been drunk, Mr. Copland pointed out the legend over the platform "Success to the Sheppey Light Railway" (applause), and said that a great amount of trouble had been expended in getting the light railway in Sheppey. The efforts of the promoters had, however, been ably seconded by the directors of the South Eastern and Chatham Railway; in fact, it was only through them that had enabled a probability — and an extreme probability — to become what they had seen that day.

Mr. Copland then went on to criticise the original plans as laid down by Holman F. Stephens in the following rather unfortunate manner:-

The plans as drawn up by the engineers — what stupid people these engineers were sometimes! — was to take the railway through the southern marshes, where scarcely a building was to be found, and this had to be deviated into the more fertile regions of the Island they had seen that day.

After speeches from Col. Boughley, Mr. Cosmo Bonsor, Mr. Vincent Hill, and Mr. A. W. Howe, the luncheon drew to a close with the singing of the National Anthem.

One of the first engines to work the line was 'Sondes' class 2-4-0T No. 518, seen here in the bay at Queenborough Station before departing to Leysdown. Dave Gilbert Collection

# OPENING OF SHEPPEY LIGHT RAILWAY.

This new Railway, which extends from Queenboro' to Leysdown, will be opened for Passenger and Goods Traffic on Thursday, August 1st, 1901, and will be worked by a Local Service from and to Queenboro' as under:—

| Distance. | DOWN.—Week-days. | a.m. | a.m. | p.m. | GDs. | p.m. | | a.m. | p.m. | p.m. | p.m. | |
|---|---|---|---|---|---|---|---|---|---|---|---|---|
| M.CHS. | | | | | | | | | Sundays. | | | |
| — | Queenboro' ......dep. | 9 5 | 11 5 | 2 5 | 4 20 | 6 40 | | 11 35 | 2 10 | 4 0 | 6 15 | ... |
| 1 39 | Sheerness East... ,, | 9 11 | 11 11 | 2 11 | 4 30 | 6 46 | Callsif required. | 11 41 | 2 16 | 4 6 | 6 21 | ... |
| 2 44 | E. Minster-on-Sea ,, | ... | ... | ... | ... | ... | | ... | ... | ... | ... | ... |
| 3 10 | Minster............ ,. | 9 18 | 11 18 | 2 18 | 4 40 | 6 53 | | 11 48 | 2 23 | 4 13 | 6 28 | ... |
| 3 79 | Brambledown Sdg ,, | ... | ... | ... | CR | ... | | ... | ... | ... | ... | ... |
| 4 73 | Grove Siding ...., | ... | ... | ... | CR | ... | | ... | ... | ... | ... | ... |
| 5 47 | Eastchurch ......:. ,,. | 9 28 | 11 28 | 2 28 | 5 0 | 7 3 | | 11 58 | 2 33 | 4 23 | 6 33 | ... |
| 6 52 | Holford Siding... ,, | ... | ... | ... | CR | ... | | ... | ... | ... | ... | ... |
| 7 7 | Harty Road Sdg. ,, | ... | ... | ... | CR | ... | CR | ... | ... | ... | ... | ... |
| 8 52 | Leysdown........ arr. | 9 40 | 11 40 | 2 40 | 5 15 | 7 15 | | 12 10 | 2 45 | 4 35 | 6 45 | ... |

| M. CHS. | UP.—Week-days. | a.m. | p.m. | GDs. | p.m. | p.m. | | p.m. | p.m. | p.m. | p.m. | |
|---|---|---|---|---|---|---|---|---|---|---|---|---|
| | | | | | | | | | Sundays. | | | |
| — | Leysdown .. ......dep | 10 0 | 12 15 | 2 50 | 5 40 | 7 30 | | 12 30 | 2 55 | 5 10 | 7 45 | ... |
| 1 45 | Harty Road Sdg ,, | ... | ... | CR | ... | ... | Callsif required. | ... | ... | ... | ... | ... |
| 2 0 | Holford Siding... ,, | ... | ... | CR | ... | ... | | ... | ... | ... | ... | ... |
| 3 5 | Eastchurch ...... ,, | 10 12 | 12 27 | 3 10 | 5 52 | 7 42 | | 12 42 | 3 7 | 5 22 | 7 57 | ... |
| 3 59 | Grove Siding ... ,, | ... | ... | CR | ... | ... | | ... | ... | ... | ... | ... |
| 4 53 | Brambledown Sdg ,, | ... | ... | CR | ... | ... | | ... | ... | ... | ... | ... |
| 5 42 | Minster............ ,, | 10 22 | 12 37 | 3 30 | 6 2 | 7 52 | | 12 52 | 3 17 | 5 32 | 8 7 | ... |
| 6 8 | E.Minster-on-Sea ,, | ... | ... | ... | ... | ... | | ... | ... | ... | ... | ... |
| 7 12 | Sheerness East... ,, | 10 29 | 12 44 | 3 40 | 6 9 | 7 59 | | 12 59 | 3 24 | 5 39 | 8 14 | ... |
| 8 52 | Queenboro' ...... arr. | 10 35 | 12 50 | 3 50 | 6 15 | 8 5 | | 1 5 | 3 30 | 5 45 | 8 20 | ... |

The Trains will run from and to a Bay Road alongside the Up Platform at Queenboro' Station.

The Line is a Single Line, with Run-Round Loops at Queenboro', Eastchurch and Leysdown, and will be worked on the Train Staff and Ticket System as under:—

| BETWEEN. | SHAPE AND COLOUR OF TRAIN STAFF. | COLOUR OF TRAIN TICKET. |
|---|---|---|
| Queenboro' and Eastchurch | { Triangular Brass Bar, Painted Red } | Red. |
| Eastchurch and Leysdown | { Round Brass Bar, Painted Green } | Blue |

These Train Staffs are necessary to unlock the Siding Points at the various Stations and Sidings, and any Train having work to do at any of the Sidings must always have the proper Train Staff, and must not be sent out with a Ticket.
The ordinary Rules for Working Single Line by Train Staff and Ticket will apply.

No Engine, Carriage, Wagon or other Vehicle (whether Loaded or Empty) whose weight exceeds 14 Tons on any pair of wheels must be used on this Light Railway.

At present the short Platform at East Minster-on-Sea, on the Up side of the Line, about midway between Sheerness East and Minster, will only be used on specified occasions, of which due notice will be given to Engineman and Guard.

The inaugural timetable.

11

After the line was opened, Holman F. Stephens wrote the following letter to his father:

8th August 1901

My dear Dah,

Many thanks for your postcard. I am very glad to hear that you & Mam have again got to a place which you like so well & which does you so much good.

I suppose Port Isaac is full of visitors and I have no doubt but that you are having grand weather.

My little Sheppey Railway was opened for traffic on 1st August but it is too early yet to say how the traffic will turnout.

The SE&CRly are working the line so that I have not much to do with the arrangements as I am only Engineer.

The Rother Valley traffic is increasing well & so is the Chichester traffic. We are not affected by coal or labour troubles as our undertakings are so small.

Hoping to see you both soon & with love to both,

I remain,

Your affectionate son.

The station building at Queenborough which was built in 1860. A six-wheeled vestibuled carriage can be seen in the Sheppey Light Railway bay (right). Lens of Sutton

A train waits at Sheerness East Station before departing for Queenborough. Author's Collection

As already mentioned, East Minster-on-Sea Station was built when the line was constructed but was at first only used on special occasions. Some of these special occasions were when the Land Company of 68 Cheapside, London E.C., who had purchased about 1000 acres of land in the Minster district, and hoped to develop the area into a seaside and health resort by selling plots to perspective buyers by running special through trains from London and carrying about 150 passengers at a time. These sales were organised by Mr. George Ramuz, a land agent who had set up an Estate Office adjoining the station under the management of Mr. Louis Ramuz.

In 1905 the SE&CR absorbed the line which was to become the only light railway in their network and decided to use a Steam Railcar for passenger service. With this in mind, wooden platforms were added to the sidings at Brambledown and Harty Road which resulted in both these places becoming Halts.

**7906**

S. E. & C. R. (SeeBack
LAND SALE.
Eastminster to
HOLBORN VIADUCT
Third 3/6
Available by the Special
Land Sale Train ONLY

S. E. & C. R. (See Back
LAND SALE
Holborn Viadnct to
EASTMINSTER
3/6 Third
Available by the Special
Land Sale Train ONLY

**7906**

Ticket dated Sept 20th 1905.
G. R. Croughton Collection

The very basic station at East Minster-on-Sea, looking towards Sheerness East soon after the line had opened.                                                                                 Author's Collection

Minster-on-Sea Station, looking towards Eastchurch. This view shows a platelayer's pump trolley with what looks like an inspection by railway officials.                          Author's Collection

In 1909 the Aero Club set up their flying grounds at Leysdown and the Short Brothers based their factory at Shellbeach, before both concerns moved to a permanent home at Eastchurch. This site was just south of Eastchurch Station and in 1911 the Royal Naval Aviation School was established on part of the Aero Club's ground.

During the 1914-18 war it was decided by the Government that a siding should be built from Eastchurch Station into the Royal Naval Aviation School and it was also agreed that the SE&CR would be responsible for the line's operation.

In September 1917, the line was out of action for nearly a whole day when a bomb fell on to the track near Sheerness East Station.

After the 1923 grouping, the line passed into the hands of the Southern Railway who increased the weight limit from 14 tons maximum to $15\frac{1}{2}$ tons.

In 1938 they also investigated the possibility of building a holiday camp at Leysdown to accommodate the many campers who frequented the Leysdown area in the summer months, but like the hotel which was proposed at the time the line was opened, this scheme also failed to materialise.

After the Second World War the railway continued to serve the Isle of Sheppey but it became obvious that it was uneconomical in many ways. It still offered that all important link with the main network at Queenborough, but when farmers began to rely more on road transport it came as no great surprise when British Railways Southern Region who had inherited the Southern Railway after nationalisation in 1948, announced its intention to close the line for passengers and goods traffic on and from Monday December 4th 1950. The final day's service was on Saturday December 2nd 1950.

Eastchurch Station soon after the line had opened. Railway Magazine

An unusual view of Leysdown Station. Author's Collection

Leysdown Station in about 1905. Lens of Sutton

14

# Description of the Route

The ancient borough of Queenborough stands on a spot which was selected by Edward III for a castle which he named Queenborough in honour of his queen, Phillipa. After the castle had been demolished, only the moat remained and even part of this was altered when the Sittingbourne and Sheerness Railway was constructed. As mentioned earlier, after the coming of the railway, Queenborough had high hopes of becoming a channel port and the SE&CR ran a day and night train service connecting with the boats at Queenborough Pier that ran to and from Flushing in Holland.

The Sheppey Light Railway started its route from a bay at the back of the up platform at Queenborough and faced north towards Sheerness.

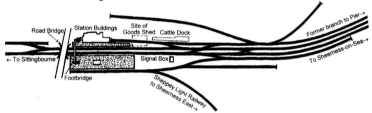

## QUEENBOROUGH STATION

Looking from the footbridge at Queenborough Station with articulated carriage set No. 514 and a parcel van in the Sheppey Light Railway bay on the right. February 4th 1950.        Denis Cullum

From Queenborough the single line quickly turned away north east towards the centre of the island across flat country which was formerly undrained marshland. After travelling for a short while, the line crossed the main Sheerness Road (now the A250) at an area known as Halfway Houses and arrived at Sheerness East Station just 1½ miles from Queenborough. Sheerness East was in fact about a mile from the main town of Sheerness but had been connected by the previously mentioned 3ft 6in gauge electric tramway which was built in 1903 but which only existed until 1917.

15

At Sheerness East, the single station platform and building was on the down side and was typical of the type of corrugated construction which Holman F. Stephens favoured on all the lines which he was involved with. The layout was completed with a goods yard of three short sidings and cattle pens.

**SHEERNESS EAST STATION**

Sheerness East Station looking towards Queenborough. November 1950. S. C. Nash

From here, low tree topped ridges appeared on both sides of the line with gradients of 1 in 89 up and 1 in 170 down, 1 in 75 up and 1 in 100 down. After passing over the Scrapsgate Road level crossing, East Minster-on-Sea Station was reached which was 2¹/₂ miles from Queenborough. Here the very name of the station was misleading as the area is really to the west of Minster-on-Sea, but as there is a West Minster between Sheerness and Queenborough, it was no doubt given the name East Minster to save any confusion.

The station was on the up side and the small primitive corrugated iron shelter resembled more the later wooden built shelters at Brambledown and Harty Road Halts than the typical Holman F. Stephens' type buildings at the other stations. The short single platform at the time the line opened was soon extended by the SE&CR. Also, East Minster-on-Sea was the only station or halt on the line without any sidings.

**EAST MINSTER-ON-SEA STATION**

East Minster-on-Sea Station looking towards Minster-on-Sea.

From the station at East Minster-on-Sea the line crossed the main Minster Road (now the B2008) on the level and at an angle and climbed a 1 in 75 and 1 in 254 up until it passed over the Scocles Road by another level crossing and arrived at Minster-on-Sea Station, which was 3$\frac{1}{2}$ miles from Queenborough.

When the line was opened, the station was just called Minster Station and the line's rule book stated that all entries i.e. goods, parcels etc., were to refer to it as Minster (Sheppey) as distinct from Minster Junction (Thanet). No doubt re-naming the station Minster-on-Sea overcame this problem.

As mentioned in the history of the line, there were ambitious plans to develop the whole area of Minster. One of these plans was for a 7000 feet long pier to be built so that pleasure steamboats running from London in the summer months would stop on their way to places like Margate. The pier was never built and the high hopes for the area were never really to materialise.

The single platform station at Minster-on-Sea was on the down side and the building was corrugated iron like Sheerness East. Sidings which at times were worked by tow rope and cattle pens completed the layout.

Minster-on-Sea Station looking towards Brambledown Halt. February 4th 1950.

17

Level Crossing   Station Building

←To East Minster-on-Sea

To Brambledown Halt→

Cattle Pens

## MINSTER-ON-SEA STATION

From Minster-on-Sea the line climbed steadily up a 1 in 70 while running along a slight embankment, before passing over Stickfast Lane level crossing and then steeply down a 1 in 74 until it reached Brambledown Halt which was 4 miles from Queenborough. At Brambledown a farm siding had been provided when the line was first opened but the wooden stilted platform and waiting shelter were added on the down side in 1905 when the Steam Railcars first used the line.

A train on the slight embankment between Minster-on-Sea and Brambledown Halt.

Jeremy Segrove Collection

Waiting Shelter   To Eastchurch→
Hut

←To Minster-on-Sea

Level Crossing

## BRAMBLEDOWN HALT

Brambledown Halt looking towards Minster-on-Sea. February 4th 1950.   Denis Cullum

On leaving Brambledown Halt the line crossed over the main road to Leysdown (now the B2231) by level crossing and then dropped at a 1 in 258 and 1 in 80 over the Newhook Farm level crossing and then took on a climb once more when gradients of 1 in 84 and 1 in 154 up were experienced before passing Grove Siding at Grove Farm which was 5 miles from Queenborough before reaching Eastchurch Station which was $5^1/_2$ miles from Queenborough.

Although it had a fully signalled loop, Eastchurch Station only had a single platform which was on the down side even though Major J. W. Pringle for the Board of Trade had requested that a second platform should be added if the station was to be used as a passing place for passenger trains. The station building was the same type of corrugated iron construction as Sheerness East and Minster-on-Sea and there were two long sidings and a cattle pen. There was also the private siding into the airfield where the Eastchurch RAF Camp and earlier flying pioneers made good use of the railway facilities.

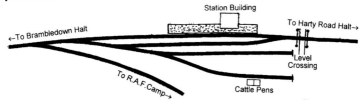

## EASTCHURCH STATION

Eastchurch Station looking towards Harty Road Halt.        Lens of Sutton

On leaving Eastchurch the line passed over a level crossing and continued climbing at 1 in 73 and 1 in 236 before reaching the summit of the line and slowly dropping until it passed Holford Siding which was on the south side of the line, 6½ miles from Queenborough. The line continued dropping in gradients until it arrived at Harty Road Halt, 7 miles from Queenborough. Like Brambledown Halt, the wooden platform and waiting shelter at Harty Road were added in 1905 and both were very similar to look at, although at Harty Road the platform was on the up side.

The line then once more crossed over the main road to Leysdown (now the B2231) on the level and passed the siding on the south side of the line. At this point a road leading south to the Harty Ferry left the main road which was to give the halt its name.

## HARTY ROAD HALT

19

Harty Road Halt looking towards Leysdown.                                          Lens of Sutton

From the siding at Harty Road Halt the line continued down gradients of 1 in 128, 540 and 223 and then passing over the level crossing at Mustards Road and a slow climb up a 1 in 660 and 97 and crossed over the Frog's Island level crossing and finally arriving at the terminus station at Leysdown, 8¾ miles from Queenborough.

Leysdown Station consisted of a single platform, a corrugated station building like Sheerness East, Minster-on-Sea and Eastchurch plus a run round loop, cattle pen and sidings. There was also a water tank which was fed from a well and worked by a wind pump. When the well was being bored it was said that the engineers struck hard rock just below the surface and the rods were diverted horizontally until they suddenly appeared some distance away, having turned in a 'U' shape.

The rods were straightened and the next time the engineers were more successful and the well was reached.

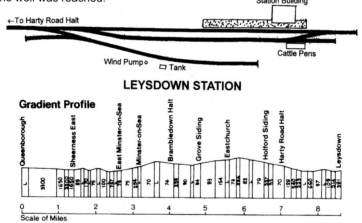

**LEYSDOWN STATION**

Gradient Profile

Scale of Miles

Leysdown Station.                                                                   Lens of Sutton

# Motive Power and Rolling Stock

Although the SE&CR did not absorb the Sheppey Light Railway until 1905, it was worked by them from the opening, so it is not so surprising that some interesting old London, Chatham & Dover Railway engines based at Sheerness Dockyard shed should be used in the first few years.

The first engine to work over the line was believed to have been a Neilson built "Scotchmen" class 0-4-2WT[*] of 1866 and some of the even earlier built R & W Hawthorn "Sondes" class 2-4-0T engines of 1857 were used in the early days.

In 1903 it was decided by the SE&CR that certain branch lines and short distance passenger services were not profitable so it was agreed that a series of trials should take place on the Sheppey Light Railway with two small petrol-electric railcars offered free of charge by Dick, Kerr & Co.

In late September 1903 they started running from Queenborough to Leysdown but because of starting trouble on cold mornings they often needed a steam locomotive to provide hot water for the radiators and also for a push start.

One of the railcars only carried four passengers and was obviously unsuitable, but the other one carried eighteen and gave a good account of itself. If a suitably qualified internal combustion engine fitter could have been engaged at Sheerness (they were few and far between at the time), the larger railcar could well have been purchased.

Because of these difficulties, Harry S. Wainwright the SE&CR Locomotive, Carriage and Wagon Superintendent designed the Steam Railcar which was an engine and carriage all in one.

The first two Steam Railcars were received at Ashford Works early in 1905, the engine portions being built by Kitson & Co. and the carriage portions were built by the Metropolitan Carriage & Wagon Co, Ltd.

At about this time an "Aeolus" class 4-4-0 had been working the line, but after Steam Railcar No. 1 had worked short trials between Dover and Deal and also over the New Romney branch it arrived at Sheerness for work on the Sheppey Light Railway. A six-wheel trailer carriage was also kept at Sheerness in case extra accommodation was called for.

[*] This information comes from a conversation that railway author and photographer R. C. Riley had with Walter 'Jack' Buddle on the very last train in 1951. Mr. Buddle was a guest of honour as it was understood that he drove the first train from Queenborough to Leysdown and back. Some reports say that Mr. Buddle in fact drove the first inspection train which hauled a directors saloon to Leysdown and back. The saloon was later taken to Chatham where it was attached to the rear of an up express.

"Scotchmen" class 0-4-2WT No. 93. It was one of this class of locomotives which worked the first train on the line.

Author's Collection

Because the Steam Railcar was introduced to lower the costs, a trial on the Sheppey Light Railway commenced between No. 1 and "Sondes" class 2-4-0T No. 523 and a train of three six-wheel carriages. The outcome was as follows:-

|  | Cost per mile | Coal burnt per mile |
|---|---|---|
| Railcar | £1.25 | 15.2 lb |
| Train | £2.08 | 26.8 lb |

In view of these figures, Wainwright was able to purchase a further six Steam Railcars of which the engine portions were again built by Kitsons, but this time the carriage portions were built by the Oldbury Carriage & Wagon Co. Ltd. Steam Railcar No. 6 was later to replace No. 1 on the Sheppey Light Railway.

Because a Steam Railcar was now working the passenger service, it was decided by the SE&CR that a light tank engine to work the goods service was required, so the unusual step was taken of ordering a "Terrier" class 0-6-0 tank engine No. 654 formally No. 54 and originally called "Waddon" from the London, Brighton & South Coast Railway.

This engine arrived at Sheerness ready for work and renumbered SE&CR No. 751 on May 24th 1905 and soon became a firm favourite on the island where it received the nickname of "Little Tich" after Harry Relph who was a 'Man of Kent' and was all the rage on the music halls at the time.

Steam Railcar No. 1.

Stroudley Terrier 0-6-0T No. 751 which was nicknamed "Little Tich" on the Sheppey Light Railway.

By 1909, because water shortages at Leysdown in the summer months led to the use of a Stirling 'O' class 0-6-0 on the daily goods service, the "Terrier" was no longer required and after a new boiler was fitted, it was moved on to Dover to relieve the Steam Railcar working on the Sandgate Branch.

The limited success of the Steam Railcars led Wainwright to proposing in November 1907 the introduction of a separate tank engine and motor train equipped carriages for branch and local duties, the result being the 'P' class 0-6-0T engines which after trials on the New Romney branch were put to good use on several branch and secondary lines. In September 1910, No. 27 of this class arrived to work the line and replace the Steam Railcar.

A "Large Scotchmen" 0-4-2WT spent its final years at Sheerness where it worked the line before being condemned in December 1913. In 1914 the Steam Railcar briefly returned.

During the 1914-18 war, the Stirling 'O' class 0-6-0 which was still handling the goods service, not only found itself working extra goods duties for the recently constructed Royal Naval Air Station at Eastchurch but also took on the passenger service as well.

In the early 1920s a Stirling 'Q' class 0-4-4 took over the passenger service but in December 1922 when the ship S.S. Gyp collided with the Kingsferry Bridge and put road and rail links with the main land out of action, the Sheppey Light Railway found itself without any locomotive power as there had not been any engines at Sheerness overnight.

Help came in the shape of an 0-6-0 saddle tank called "Emerald Isle" which was borrowed from Settle & Speakman of Queenborough who had their own private siding south of Queenborough Station. After about two months, two 'P' class 0-6-0T engines were dismantled and sent to the island by boat, where apart from other duties they worked the Sheppey Light Railway.

When things returned to normal the line was to see the Sharp Stewart built 'R' and 'R1' class 0-4-4 tanks which were to work the line right up to the closure in December 1950.

During this time, Stirling 'B1' class 4-4-0s and Wainwright 'E' class 4-4-0s were occasionally seen working the line.

The goods service in the later years was handled by the ever hard working Wainwright 'C' class 0-6-0 engines who like the previously mentioned Stirling 'O' class 0-6-0s were sometimes used for passenger work as well.

'Sondes' class 2-4-0T No. 520 waiting for passengers at East Minster-on-Sea. Lens of Sutton

Steam Railcar No. 1 waiting in the bay platform at Queenborough Station. R. L. Ratcliffe Collection

B1 class 4-4-0 No. 1021 at Leysdown Station in August 1936.     L&GPR Collection

(*Above left*) E class 4-4-0 No. 1157 at Sheerness East Station. July 1st 1950.     D. Trevor Rowe
(*Above right*) C class 0-6-0 No. 1252 crossing over the Scrapsgate Road. June 2nd 1936. H. F. Wheeller

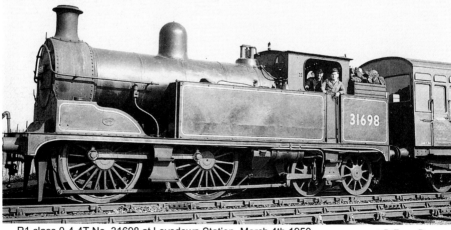

R1 class 0-4-4T No. 31698 at Leysdown Station. March 4th 1950.     D. Trevor Rowe

Rolling stock on the line originally consisted of three London, Chatham & Dover Railway six-wheel saloon carriages which were built in 1887 and were fitted with vestibules and low footboards. They were to remain in service until 1924 when they were converted to four-wheelers and sent to the Isle of Wight.

From this time onwards the carriage portions of Steam Railcar Nos. 1, 2, 3 and 8 were paired as two articulated sets for use on the Sheppey Light Railway and were numbered 3561 and 976 to form set No. 514 and 3660 and 975 forming set No. 513. These two sets had the distinction of being the only articulated stock operated by the Southern Railway who had inherited the line at the time of grouping. When the line closed in December 1950, set No. 514 was transferred to the Portland branch in Dorset and after that branch closed in March 1952 the set moved on to the Exmouth branch. In August 1952, set No. 514 went to join set No. 513 on the Clapham Junction – Kensington service.

Sheppey Light Railway carriage nameboard. June 2nd 1936.                                    H. F. Wheeller

Close-up view of the articulated carriage bogie set of No. 514. June 2nd 1936.                                    H. F. Wheeller

The train at Leysdown Station. June 2nd 1936.                                    H. F. Wheeller

Passenger and goods trains pass at Eastchurch Station. October 8th 1948.                                    W. A. Camwell

# Signalling and Light Railway Working

From the outset the line was worked on the train staff and ticket principle, comprising two blocks:- Queenborough to Eastchurch and Eastchurch to Leysdown.

The shape and colour of the staff for the Queenborough to Eastchurch section was a triangular brass bar which was painted red while the Eastchurch to Leysdown section was a round brass bar painted green. The staff was of course used to unlock the sidings points at the stations, halts and also the sidings at Grove and Holford.

The colour of the Queenborough to Eastchurch train ticket was red and the Eastchurch to Leysdown section was blue.

Communications along the line were by telephone which meant that trains were signalled from station to station. The signal "Is line clear?", "Train in section" and "Train cleared" were given verbally over the phone. Signals were provided at the block stations and were worked by ground frames by the station staff after the proper procedure had been taken on the telephone and the "Line clear" signal had been given and acknowledged.

The level crossing gates at the stations were also worked by the station staff but otherwise were worked by the guard of the train who would also issue the tickets in tram conductor style. The farm and accommodation level crossings that did not have gates were provided with cattle grids.

The guard working the crossing gates at Brambledown Halt. June 2nd 1936.    H. F. Wheeller

The same guard entering one of the carriages to issue tickets. June 2nd 1936.    H. F. Wheeller

# Timetables and Tickets

## SUMMER 1937

**QUEENBOROUGH and LEYSDOWN (One class only).**

| Miles | Down. | Week Days. mrn | mrn | mrn | aft | aft | aft SX | aft SO | aft WSO | Sundays mrn | aft | aft | aft |
|---|---|---|---|---|---|---|---|---|---|---|---|---|---|
| | Queenborough..dep. | 6 44 | 8 16 | 11 4 | 2 20 | 4 4 | 6 55 | 7 8 | 10 35 | 1045 | 2 35 | 5 40 | 8 5 |
| 1¼ | Sheerness East...... | 6 49 | 8 20 | 11 8 | 2 24 | 4 8 | 6 59 | 7 12 | 10 39 | 1049 | 2 39 | 5 44 | 8 9 |
| 2¼ | East Minster-on-Sea | 6 56 | 8 26 | 1114 | 2 30 | 4 15 | 7 8 | 7 25 | 10 46 | 1055 | 2 45 | 5 50 | 8 15 |
| 3¼ | Minster-on-Sea...... | 7 0 | 8 30 | 1118 | 2 34 | 4 19 | 7 13 | 7 30 | 10 52 | 11 1 | 2 51 | 5 56 | 8 21 |
| 4½ | Brambledown Halt. | 7 4 | 8 34 | 1122 | 2 38 | 4 22 | 7 17 | 7 32 | 10 57 | 11 5 | 2 55 | 6 0 | 8 25 |
| 5¼ | Eastchurch.......... | 7 10 | 8 40 | 1127 | 2 43 | 4 28 | 7 23 | 7 38 | 11 3 | 1111 | 3 1 | 6 6 | 8 31 |
| 7 | Harty Road Halt... | 7 17 | 8 44 | 1132 | 2 48 | 4 33 | 7 29 | 7 44 | 11 7 | 1117 | 3 7 | 6 12 | 8 37 |
| 8¼ | Leysdown......arr. | 7 23 | 8 51 | 1138 | 2 54 | 4 39 | 7 35 | 7 50 | 11 13 | 1123 | 3 13 | 6 18 | 8 43 |

| Miles | Up. | Week Days. mrn | mrn | mrn | aft | aft | aft | aft WSO | Sundays aft | aft | aft | aft | |
|---|---|---|---|---|---|---|---|---|---|---|---|---|---|
| | Leysdown ......dep. | 7 30 | 9 5 | 1146 | 3 0 | 5 0 | 7 55 | 11 20 | 1 0 | 3 55 | 7 5 | 8 55 | .. |
| 1¼ | Harty Road Halt.... | 7 34 | 9 9 | 1150 | 3 4 | 5 L13 | 7 59 | 11 24 | 1 4 | 3 59 | 7 9 | 8 59 | ... |
| 3½ | Eastchurch........... | 7 39 | 9 14 | 1155 | 3 9 | 5 21 | 8 4 | 11 29 | 1 8 | 4 3 | 7 13 | 9 3 | .. |
| 4½ | Brambledown Halt.. | 7 44 | 9 19 | 12 1 | 3 14 | 5 32 | 8 11 | 11 35 | 1 16 | 4 11 | 7 21 | 9 11 | .. |
| 5¼ | Minster-on-Sea...... | 7 48 | 9 23 | 12 5 | 3 18 | 5 36 | 8 15 | 11 39 | 1 21 | 4 16 | 7 26 | 9 16 | .. |
| 6½ | East Minster-on-Sea. | 7 51 | 9 26 | 12 8 | 3 21 | 5 39 | 8 18 | 11 42 | 1 24 | 4 19 | 7 29 | 9 19 | ... |
| 7½ | Sheerness East..[359 | 7 58 | 9 33 | 1215 | 3 28 | 5 46 | 8 25 | 11 49 | 1 30 | 4 25 | 7 35 | 9 25 | .. |
| 8¼ | Queenborough..arr. | 8 4 | 9 39 | 1221 | 3 34 | 5 52 | 8 31 | 11 55 | 1 36 | 4 31 | 7 42 | 9 31 | ... |

L Arr 5 5 aft  SO Saturdays only  SX Saturdays excepted
WSO Wednesdays and Saturdays only

## SUMMER 1950

**QUEENBOROUGH and LEYSDOWN—Third class only**

| Miles | Down | Week Days only a.m | a.m | a.m | | a.m | | p.m |
|---|---|---|---|---|---|---|---|---|
| | Queenborough..... dep | 6 30 | 8 16 | 1055 | Saturdays excepted | 11 4 | Saturdays only | 4 22 |
| 1½ | Sheerness East......... | 6 35 | 8 21 | 11 0 | | 11 9 | | 4 27 |
| 2½ | East Minster-on-Sea... | 6 42 | 8 27 | 11 6 | | 1115 | | 4 33 |
| 3½ | Minster-on-Sea ........ | 6 45 | 8 31 | 1110 | | 1119 | | 4 37 |
| 4½ | Brambledown Halt.... | 6 50 | 8 35 | 1114 | | 1123 | | 4 41 |
| 5½ | Eastchurch............. | 6 57 | 8 41 | 1119 | | 1129 | | 4 47 |
| 7 | Harty Road Halt....... | 7 3 | 8 45 | 1124 | | 1133 | | 4 52 |
| 8¾ | Leysdown.......... arr | 7 9 | 8 52 | 1130 | | 1139 | | 4 57 |

| Miles | Up | Week days only a.m | a.m | a.m | | a.m | | p.m |
|---|---|---|---|---|---|---|---|---|
| | Leysdown .......... dep | 7 15 | 9 5 | 1136 | Saturdays excepted | 1145 | Saturdays only | 5 5 |
| 1¾ | Harty Road Halt....... | 7 20 | 9 10 | 1141 | | 1150 | | 5 10 |
| 3¼ | Eastchurch.............. | 7 25 | 9 15 | 1146 | | 1155 | | 5 15 |
| 4½ | Brambledown Halt .... | 7 30 | 9 20 | 1151 | | 12 0 | | 5 20 |
| 5¼ | Minster-on-Sea ........ | 7 34 | 9 24 | 1155 | | 12 4 | | 5 24 |
| 6½ | East Minster-on-Sea.... | 7 37 | 9 27 | 1158 | | 12 7 | | 5 27 |
| 7½ | Sheerness East......... | 7 44 | 9 34 | 12 5 | | 1214 | | 5 34 |
| 8½ | Queenborough .... arr | 7 49 | 9 39 | 1210 | | 1219 | | 5 39 |

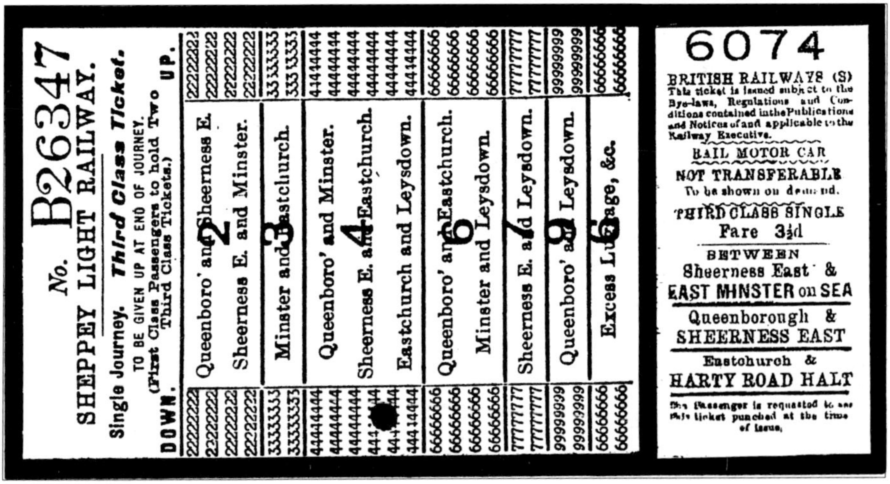


(*Above left*) Early Sheppey Light Railway ticket (actual size). Note that 1st class passengers were issued with two third class tickets. Col. Stephens Railways Museum, Tenterden (*Above right*) A typical example of a British Railways ticket issued in the last few years. G. R. Croughton Collection

# Life on the "Sheppey Light"

Like most light railways and rural branch lines the Sheppey Light Railway has had and will no doubt continue to have, many stories told about it, some true and some not so true, but all told in good faith and humour.

One such story was when the late Mr. Charles Love (senior) who had a farm near Brambledown Halt was on his way from Queenborough to Brambledown Halt after crossing over the Scrapsgate Road where the guard had to get down to open and close the gates, the train moved on about a hundred yards and then stopped. After a while Mr. Love put his head out of the window and asked the guard (who was walking alongside the carriage) what the trouble was. "Cow on the line" was the answer. The train continued but then stopped again some two hundred yards further on. The guard descended once more and Mr. Love asked "is it another cow?" No was the guard's reply "it's the same one, caught us up and passed us".

Another interesting little story came from a Mrs. P. Harris of Sittingbourne who remembered that back in the early 1940s when she worked in the Women's Land Army and was billeted and worked at Sheppey Court where the line ran through the fields. When she used to go and get the cows in for milking, the train driver would stop his train so that she could drive the cows over the line and would also have a chat before going on his way. This would happen every day and on one occasion when a cow was trapped in a ditch, the good old "Sheppey Light" came to the rescue and pulled it out.

The late Len Hedge was a driver on the line and remembered an old man who lived in an old Army dug-out near Leysdown Station who would come up to the train crew while at Leysdown Station and "tap them up" for a bit of coal for his fire. Mr. Hedge also remembered when the train would stop at Holford siding and put down passengers for the Boxing Day Greyhound Cup.

The late Vic Martin of Warden remembered enquiring at Eastchurch Station about a chair which he had been waiting some weeks to be delivered, only to discover that the guard to whom he was talking was sitting comfortably on it and had been using it for some time.

Leysdown Station in the deep bleak winter.

Jeremy Segrove Collection

# Closure

Once the line became part of British Railways Southern Region, after nationalisation in 1948, the new owners soon decided that the "Sheppey Light" was not paying its way and announced their intention to close the line for passengers and goods traffic on and from Monday December 4th 1950.

Opposition from many local people, including the Sheerness Urban District Council to keep the line open came to nothing.

The last day's service was on Saturday, December 2nd 1950 (there had been no Sunday service for some time) and the islanders certainly turned out in full force to give the railway a grand but somewhat sad send off.

The last train to leave Queenborough for Leysdown was the 4.27 p.m. which was made up of 'R1' class 0-4-4T engine No. 31705 pulling articulated carriage set No. 514 and a parcel van.

The driver was Ernest 'Tom' Birtchnell, the fireman was Don Pilcher and the guard was Edgar Cackett. Also aboard was Walter 'Jack' Buddle who had driven the very first train over the line. How unique that the first and last driver should have been together on such an occasion.

Members of the Sheppey Rural District Council were also present and were represented by Wing Comdr. W. E. James, J.P., C.C. (Chairman), Cllr. Alfred Johnson, J.P., Mr. E. F. Brading (Surveyor & Engineer).

Also aboard were members of the Light Railway Retention League together with enthusiasts from all over the country (one even cycled from Croydon) who had come to pay their last respects.

At each station on the outward journey, passengers were waiting to join the train and ride across the island for the very last time. Edgar Cackett the guard was besieged by everyone aboard who wanted tickets as souvenirs (some of the tickets were very faded!).

At Leysdown preparations had been made and members of the Parish Council and villagers combined to give the last train an unforgettable send off from the eastern side of the island.

A mock coffin draped in black was borne on the shoulders of four sturdy "mourners" who marched in a solemn procession from the village to the station.

The 'dreaded' closure poster.
G. W. Powell, courtesy R. C. Riley

Two views from an earlier train on the last day. *(Top)* Between Minster-on-Sea and Brambledown. *(Bottom)* At Eastchurch Station. December 2nd 1950. Dr. E. Course

29

The coffin which bore the inscription "R.I.P. to dear old Sheppey Light Railway — no more to trip through tulips" was placed on the train and a wreath was placed on the buffers before the last train pulled out of Leysdown Station to the sound of fireworks, bells, whistles, fog signals and car horns. *(Note: The reference to tulips refers to the fact that over the years, many tulip bulbs were scattered on the embankments along the route.)*

At each station and halt people waited to catch the train or simply wave and all along the route at lighted windows in houses, curtains were drawn open as the occupiers took their last look. At level crossing gates waiting motorists sounded their horns.

When Eastchurch was reached, the Mayor wearing his chain of office accompanied by members of the Parish Council were all waiting to join the train.

At Minster-on-Sea there was yet another demonstration as a second coffin and set of "mourners" wearing top hats boarded the train.

On leaving Sheerness East Station, buses and cars held up at the level crossing gave the train a real "blasting" on their horns as it rattled over the road for the last time.

When at last the train reached Queenborough Station, passengers crowded the platform where the "funeral parties" posed for the press cameramen.

After the coffins had been "officially" received by Ald. R. J. Jennings on behalf of the Mayor of Queenborough there was a short "burial service" where the whole crowd stood in complete silence as members of the St. John's Ambulance Cadets sounded the "Last Post".

Later, when No. 31705 had put the empty stock in the siding and a train had left for Sheerness-on-Sea followed by another one to Sittingbourne, the crowd had gone and the station at Queenborough was quiet.

And so the Sheppey Light Railway was finished, no more to run across those low fields above the marsh and through the gently rolling hills of the island's centre, never again would the sound of the whistle be heard as the train approached an ungated level crossing. In fact, no more to trip through tulips.

(*Above left*) The last train at Queenborough Station after arriving with 'mourners' and mock coffins. Standing on the front of the engine are Walter 'Jack' Buddle (left) the first driver on the line in 1901, Ernest 'Tom' Birtchnell (centre) the last driver, and Don Pilcher (right) fireman. December 2nd 1950. G. W. Powell, courtesy R. C. Riley (*Above right*) A similar view. Jeremy Segrove Collection

# The Present Scene

To look for what remains of the line today is a difficult but interesting task as much of the former route has been reclaimed by farmers or built on by developers.

At Queenborough the bay platform has been filled in and there are no visible signs of the "Sheppey Light".

At the site of Sheerness East, the single platform remained for many years even while it was in use as a Council Yard. The whole area has now been developed and features a housing estate off Power Station Road (the name coming from the former Tram Station), with some very interesting road names, William Rigby Drive, Buddle Drive, and finally Scotchmen Close. As previously mentioned, all very much names from the history of the Sheppey Light Railway.

From here onwards, fragmented bits and pieces of the very overgrown route can still be spotted by a very keen eye, but there is no trace of East Minster-on-Sea Station which is now a residential area. From here it is hard to imagine that there was ever a level crossing over the main road to Minster (now the B2008).

At Scocles Road there is no sign of the level crossing which adjoined Minster-on-Sea Station and there are no remains of the station.

The slight embankment that marks the route from Minster-on-Sea towards Brambledown Halt is still visible on leaving the site of Minster-on-Sea Station, but towards Brambledown it seems to disappear.

The site of Brambledown Halt is very hard to locate as a bungalow has now been built on the very spot although the wooden platform shelter was saved and was put to good use by the village cricket club at Eastchurch.

From Brambledown to Eastchurch there is very little to see and the site of Eastchurch Station is very overgrown.

The former RAF Station at Eastchurch later became a Borstal Institution and some of the inmates were reputed to have helped in the removal of the railway tracks. The Borstal later became a Prison. On leaving Eastchurch the route is very overgrown.

At the site of Harty Road Halt one would never know that the small wooden platform and shelter ever existed, but the telephone poles and wire do give a clue to the alignment of the railway. The shelter from Harty Road Halt was also saved and later found use as a shed at Kings Hill Farm on Elmley Island.

From Harty Road the overgrown route is still visible and can be traced most of the way to Leysdown where the site of the station is still a wide open expanse and is now a car park while little remains to remind people that it was at one time the terminus of the Sheppey Light Railway. Standing in the area today it's very difficult to imagine what it was like on the day the line closed on December 2nd 1950 when the last train left Leysdown and it's even harder to imagine what it must have been like on August 9th 1901 when John Copland and his guests stood on the platform with such high hopes for the railway's future.

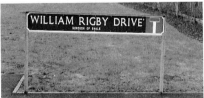 

(*Above left*) William Rigby Drive on the site of Sheerness East Station. (*Above right*) The car park on the site of Leysdown Station. Both photographs taken on December 23rd 2002.  Author

# Conclusion

Looking back, the Sheppey Light Railway did serve the Isle of Sheppey, but with a restricted service and improving road transport, the railway had unfortunately fulfilled its role.

Like many other light railways and country branch lines the "Sheppey Light" found itself facing the cruel world of the realist after the Second World War and was running with only a handful of passengers. This of course being the main reason that led to the closure.

If it had lasted 15 to 20 years longer, it could well have been saved by a preservation group and would have given the island a much needed tourist attraction, but this was not to be.

To stand in the centre of the island and imagine an 'R' or 'R1' class engine rattling its way through the low rolling hills with an articulated carriage set brings to mind a bygone time, a time unfortunately that will never happen again.

# Acknowledgements

I would like to thank the following people and organisations for their kind help in compiling information and supplying photographs for this publication:- Mr. D. Gilbert, Mr. D. Cullum, Mr. S. C. Nash, Mr. B. R. Hart, Mr. R. C. Riley, Mr. D. Trevor Rowe, Dr. Edwin Course, Mr. J. Segrove, Mr. G. R. Croughton, Mr. M. Hawkins, Mr. J. Scott-Morgan, Mr. D. Miles, Mr. D. Pilcher, Mr. J. Miller and Mr. P. Shaw of the Col. Stephens Museum (Tenterden), the librarians and staff at Sheerness Library, the Public Records Office at Kew and last but certainly not least the following gentlemen who are unfortunately no longer with us:- Mr. J. L. Smith (of Lens of Sutton), Mr. W. A. Camwell, Mr. H. F. Wheeler, Mr. V. Martin, Mr. L. Hedge, Mr. E. D. Bruton and Mr. G. W. Powell.

My grateful thanks to Norman Branch for reading and checking my text and also to James Christian of Binfield Printers Ltd.

# Bibliography

FORGOTTEN RAILWAYS: SOUTH-EAST ENGLAND by H. P. White (David & Charles)
THE SHEPPEY LIGHT RAILWAY by Brian Hart (Wild Swan)
THE RAILWAYS OF SOUTHERN ENGLAND: INDEPENDENT AND LIGHT RAILWAYS by Edwin Course (Batsford)
THE RAILWAY MAGAZINE (Various issues)

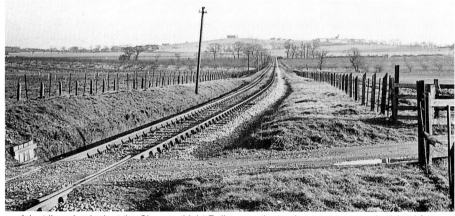

A last lingering look at the Sheppey Light Railway as the track sweeps across the island from the crossing near Newhook Farm towards Eastchurch. February 4th 1950.          Denis Cullum